# Inter~~cessory~~

# Prayers

## (Intercessors, Angelic Armies, Heavenly Warriors Divine Intervention)

IKECHUKWU JOSEPH

# DEDICATION

to all intercessors who groan day and night for the salvation of the elect. I tell you, he will give them justice quickly .

# CONTENTS

# 1 INTERCESSION DEFINED AND EXPLAINED

- That day with the whole burning zeal and hunger for God and compassion for souls we went for vigil. To intercede for world revival, for divine intervention and world evangelization. Righteousness and supernatural occurrences were common among the believers fellowship. We use to call that all night long prayers night-watch. Most times we use to pray all night. During each meeting after all other preambles, we knelt in prayers from around 10p.m. Our prayers then were mainly for salvation of souls. We hardly prayed for ourselves. I was surprised when we got up it was around 4a.m, still looking fresh. For about 6 hours, non-stop marathon prayers. We were driven by burden, passion for souls, and hunger to find God and His righteousness. Intercession is a spiritual builder. No wonder the power that followed our gathering. Sins were exposed and convicted by the Holy Spirit. Once fire gulp up a whole house and everything was done to put it off but it failed. Then our evangelist just came and commanded in the name of Jesus and the whole conflagration went off. That was God working among His people.
- There is no power like that of prevailing prayers of Abraham pleading for Sodom, Jacob wrestling in the stillness of the night; Moses standing in the breach to

protect his people, Hannah intoxicated with sorrowful groanings for a child, David heartbroken with remorse and grief or Jesus in sweat of blood.

- **Intercession Defined**: Intercession means inter alia, seeking the presence and hearing of God on behalf of others.

- Intercession is a prayer, petition, or entreaty in favor of another. It could be for individuals, nations, cities, governments, authorities or for all men or salvation of souls. Christ is continually still making intercession for us

...Who is even at the right hand of God, who also maketh intercession for us. Rom 8:34

- Several times I have been burdened to pray for someone's salvation, healing of a loved one or for some problem to receive divine attention. This night I knelt in prayers and agonized in prayers, praying in spirit for about six hours nonstop. But had to get up as I had to go to work. When the spirit of intercession comes upon you, nothing matters again. Not food, not time, not happenings in your environ, not your ego or wellbeing. When such burden persists, continue in prayers until the burden is lifted. You wouldn't even know when time is gone.

### Romans 8:26

Likewise, the Spirit also helpeth our infirmities: for we know not what we should pray for as we ought: but the Spirit itself maketh intercession for us with groanings which cannot be uttered.

- This is what the church today has lost. All the worldwide fire revivals, miracles and mass salvation of souls in the 1970s which was as a result of people praying everywhere. Today worldly entertainment has taken over and driven away the power and presence of God from the church. But God has promised us restoration. Kneeling we shall triumph over the power of darkness and the dark kingdom that has been unleashed into the world. Watchman what of the night? In 2 Chron. 7:14 the scripture says, "If my people, which are called by my name, shall:

- humble (*kâ na'* implying to bend the knees, into

2

subjection, be subdued) themselves,

- and pray (*pâ lal* meaning to intercede, intervene, intreat)

- and seek (*bâ qash* here denotes to seek to find, to seek to secure, to search out, to strive after) my face,

- and turn (*shû b* denotes to turn back to God, be restored, repent) from their wicked ways;

then will I hear from heaven, and will forgive their sins, and will heal their land. Land here reffering to the people of the land, city, tribe, country, family. These are the elements and basis of proper and true intercession. "If" is conditional and set by God to test our obedience. If, in the Bible is attached or followed by a promise or blessings if fulfilled or curse if otherwise. Wake up the sleeping Giants. Call a solemn assembly. Weep on the altars of your heart.

- Jesus continued all night in prayers when he needed to make important decisions, when he chose the 12 apostles

**Luke 6:12-13**

And it came to pass in those days, that he went out into a mountain to pray, and continued all night in prayer to God.

Amplified version of the bible puts it thus:: Now in those days it occurred that He went up into a mountain to pray, and spent the whole night in prayer to God.

13. And when it was day, he called unto him his disciples: and of them he chose twelve, whom also he named apostles...

- **Kingly intercession** is entreaties accompanied by kingly anointing. It is Intercession of a king or one in authority.

**- Keys for Kingly Intercession:**

Key (*maphtê ach* denotes opening instrument, an opener). Open doors and open heavens don't just happen. History has records of satanic strongholds - closed political systems, national siege, communist, socialist, Ishmaelite bondwoman's wild children's problems. For more on closed doors see my book, Unlocking Closed Doors.

- *And the key of the house of David I will lay upon his*

3

*shoulder; he shall open and no one shall shut, he shall shut and no one shall open (Isaiah 22:22 AMP)*

And I tell you, you are Peter [Greek, *petro* large piece of rock], and on this rock [Greek, *petra* huge rock like Gibraltar] I will build My church, and the gates of Hades (the powers of the infernal region) shall not overpower it [or be strong to its detriment or hold out against it].

I will give you the keys of the kingdom of heaven; and whatever you bind (declare to be improper and unlawful) on earth must be what is already bound in heaven; and whatever you lose (declare lawful) on earth must be what is already loosed in heaven (Matthew 16:18-19 AMP).

- **Keys, divine God ordained keys** are important in this kingdom business. A version rendered that verse 22 as "And I will give the key of the family of David into his care; and what he keeps open will be shut by no one, and what he keeps shut no one will make open"

- A priesthood of believers (Exodus 19:5-6; 1 Peter 2:
5-9)

-1 Peter 2 verse 9 called believers, a royal priesthood meaning you possess kingly and priestly authorities. Royal (basileios = royal, kingly, regal) and priesthood (hierateuma meaning office or order of priests). So much authority (delegated power) bestowed on you to rule and reign where you are planted. Psalm 110:2 says rule in the midst of your enemies.

- **All believers are called to Intercession**: Prayer and Submission to Authority. All believers in the New Testament were priests of the royal priesthood. Hence you must carry out your first duty which is interceding for all people.

**1 Tim 2:1 (AMP)**

First of all, then, I admonish and urge that petitions, prayers, intercessions, and thanksgivings be offered on behalf of all men.

EasyEnglish Version says so then, these are the most important things that I must ask you to do. Each of you should ask God to supply what others need. You must pray

4

for everyone. You must ask God to help them. And you must thank God for what he has done for everyone. I strongly ask you to do these things.

- As intercessors we can use these kingly and priestly anointings to unlock and lock spiritual doors. Our armors are not physical but spiritual. Kneeling we triumph. Victory come by bonding and losing, pulling down stronghold, winning wars and conquering kingdoms. Kings reigns, rule, have dominions and exhibit kingly anointing, a display of complete set of armors and command. By extension something that covers and protects.

Priestly Intercession:

- Vine's dictionary defined priest (Heb. *Kōhēn*) as an authorized minister of deity who officiates at the altar. He performs sacrificial, ritualistic, mediatorial duties. By contrast a prophet is an intermediary between God and the people. Since Christ offered up himself, all Jewish and gentile believers, constituted a kingdom of priests. Rev. 1:6, a holy priesthood, 1 Peter 2:5. the ministry of a priest is to offer spiritual sacrifices

- the high or chief priest once a year on the day of atonement, enters into the Holy of Holies (from which the other priests were excluded) and offer sacrifices for his own sins and the sins of the people. Christ became our High Priest by undergoing a bloody death making himself an expiatory sacrifice to God, that is an act of atonement for sin and has entered into the heavenly sanctuary where he continually intercedes on our behalf.

The priest stands between God and the people interceding with spiritual sacrifices. So, every believer and intercessor must learn consecration and sacrifice here as elements of intercession

- So, a priest-king is a sacred king, a sovereign high priest and called into the ministry of intercession and reconciliation.

**- Prophetic Intercession**

A prophet is an intermediary between God and the people.

5

Someone defined Prophetic intercessors as a prophetic, priestly army designed as guardians, dedicated to protect through prayer a specific post. They are watchmen and watchers over God's plans and patterns. He must consecrate himself to see and hear the mind of God. The intimacy with God must be strong to be trusted by God. The secret of the Lord is with them that fear him. Remember Abraham's intercession for Sodom and Gomorrah (Genesis 18). Prophetic intercession involves interceding from the mind of God about nationals, governments, authorities, communities, strategic and circumstantial grey knots and areas. Those asking for world peace, what is the mind of God in this world of crisis. Those involved in this type of intercession must shade their idiosyncrasies and be ready to go with God.

**We had a small group** where we gather once a week to pray for world revival. There were other small groups here and there in the early 1970s praying for either salvation of souls, national revival, community deliverance as God led them. The consecration, passion, burden for soul, hunger for righteousness was high that drove believers to their kneels in agony of souls. What anguish of heart will keep the young and old on their kneels for hours or all nights crying, "give me children or I die. give me souls or converts, if I perish, I perish. With fasting of food, pleasure and sleep. With self-denial and denial of self they wait on God. Some sold their cars, properties, estates and surrender proceed to God. Some even burnt their certificates to avoid distraction. They were not crazy. Of course, we know the result today. The church most go back to the basics as when we believed. A praying church is a winning church. We stop praying to start sinning and we start sinning to stop praying.

**- Urgency and Challenge of Prophetic Intercession:**
Jer. 27:18 AMP: But if they are true prophets and if the word of the Lord is really spoken by them, let them now make intercession to the Lord of hosts, that the vessels which are [still] left in the house of the Lord, in the house of the king of Judah, and in Jerusalem may not go to Babylon.

### - Joel 2:17 AMP:

Let the priests, the ministers of the Lord, weep between the porch and the altar; and let them say, have pity and spare Your people, O Lord, and give not Your heritage to reproach, that the [heathen] nations should rule over them or use a byword against them. Why should they say among the peoples, where is their God?

### Isaiah 62:6-7 AMP:

*6. I have set watchmen upon your walls, O Jerusalem, who will never hold their Peace Day or night; you who [are His servants and by your prayers] put the Lord in remembrance [of His promises], keep not silence*

*7. And give Him no rest until He establishes Jerusalem and makes her a praise in the earth.*

- When the church has become a refrigerator and grown into a stunted place and become nothing but debris and ashes. When the kindling fire no more burns because there are no oil, anointing oil. When the light has grown dim and the people no longer see clearly. When the walls, the defence and security are broken down. When the voice of God we hear no more and the silence of God become pronounced. When the rubble stones pile so high. Someone must build a hedge and stand in the gap.

### Isa. 59:16 AMP:

And He saw that there was no man and wondered that there was no intercessor [no one to intervene on behalf of truth and right]; therefore, His own arm brought Him victory, and His own righteousness [having the Spirit without measure] sustained Him.

- When the nation's national leaders and politician bring in strange gods upon their people. When occultism, idolatry, marine forces and demonic operations prevail. Where are the intercessors that will storm the heavens for divine intervention.

- where are the Jeremiahs of God to weep between the

porch and the altars? Oh, that my head were waters and my eyes a reservoir of tears, that I might weep day and night for the slain of the daughter of my people! (Jer. 9:1).

- **We were praying for a lady** that had a marine spirit covenant. At a point she was not communicating with us but rather with another host of beings. Something inside me said, Anoint her ears and tongue with oil. As I was reluctant to obey, another young convert ran to me and said he heard a voice asking us to anoint her ears and tongue. This was a confirmation of what God placed in my heart. As I anointed her, her tongue loosed and she started talking to us and was delivered. Praise God.

*****

- God is not looking for capable hands but for available vessels.

- Prayers ascends by fire. Flames give prayer access as well as winds, acceptance as well as energy. There is no incense without fire and no prayers without flame - E. M Bounds

- In lifes journey, it is better to be a supporting pillar than a destroying caterpillar.

- Before the great revival in Gallneukirvhen broke out Martin Boos spent hours days and often nights in lonely agonies of intercession ... When he preached his words were like flames - D.M McIntyre D.D

- Be filled with the Spirit - Ephesians 5:18B

# 2 GREAT INTERCESSORS

**Several members of Jonathan Edward's church** had spent the whole night in prayers before he preached his memorial sermon, sinners in the hands of an angry God. The Holy Ghost was so mightily poured out and God so manifested in holiness and majesty during the preaching of that sermon, that the elders threw their arms around the church pillars and cried, Lord save us, we are slipping down into hell. But there is a little history behind this. For three days Edward was said not to have eaten even a mouthful of food; for three nights he had not closed his eyes in sleep. Over and over again, he had been saying to God in a heavy heart; Give me New England! Give me New England. That was wrestling indeed, like the night of Jacob's encounter with God.

- An intercessor is someone who by nature or calling choose to mediate, appeal, entreat, plea, pray, supplicate on behalf of another.

### Ezek. 22:30 (NET)

I looked for a man from among them who would repair the wall and stand in the gap before me on behalf of the land, so that I would not destroy it, but I found no one.

- Culturally those days walls and gates, like the wall of

Jericho and strongholds were built around cities to protect and secure them and their inhabitants. Massive walls and gates ward off enemies. Broken walls were a risk factor. So, standing in the gap was the duty of a watchman. So spiritually speaking intercessors stand in the presence of God making intercessory prayer on behalf of others, building up hedges of protection around the weak and defenseless, destroying strongholds and setting the captives free. Just like Christ is now sitting in the presence of God interceding for us.

**- Distinguishing Features of An Intercessor**

- Intercessors are visionary persons. They see, hear and perceive the mind of God.

- Intercessors should have broken spirit.

The sacrifices of God are a broken spirit: a broken and a contrite heart, O God, thou wilt not despise. Ps 51:17

The LORD is nigh unto them that are of a broken heart; and saveth such as be of a contrite spirit. Psalm 34:18

- Intercessors have passion and love for souls

- Intercessors are not hired laborers

- Intercessors should be courageous, steadfast, and be ready to sacrifice.

- intercession goes with daily consecration, self-denial and even denial of self.

For to me to live is Christ, and to die is gain (Phil 1:21)

- Intercessors are God's watchmen, warriors and army. Shall these bones rise again - an invading army of God?

Intercession in the Old Testament

**- Hezekiah interceded for the people** for their sin of violation of the law (2 Chron. 30:18)

- Samuel interceded for Israel (1 Sam.7:9)

**- Moses interceded for healing** of Miriam for she was smitten with leprous (Num. 12:13).

**- Man of God interceded** for Restoration of the king's hand (1King 13:6).

- Ministers interceded for the people (Joel 2:17).

**- Moses, interceded for the Israelites** on different

times.

Deut. 9:18 AMP

*Then I fell down before the Lord as before, for forty days and forty nights; I neither ate food nor drank water, because of all the sin you had committed in doing wickedly in the sight of the Lord, to provoke Him to anger* (ref Deut. 9:25, Deut. 10:10).

**- Abraham, interceded for the city of Sodom.**

**- Zipporah, Moses wife**

Exo. 4:24 - 26 (AMP)

Along the way at a [resting-] place, the Lord met [Moses] and sought to kill him [made him acutely and almost fatally ill]. [Now apparently, he had failed to circumcise one of his sons, his wife being opposed to it; but seeing his life in such danger] Zipporah took a flint knife and cut off the foreskin of her son and cast it to touch [Moses] feet, and said, Surely a husband of blood you are to me! When He let [Moses] alone [to recover], Zipporah said, A husband of blood are you because of the circumcision.

- Moses's wife, Zipporah on their way to Egypt for Moses to ask Pharaoh to let God's people go, intervened when danger locked against her husband. God wanted to kill Moses but Zipporah's intervention averted the death of Moses from an angry God. Moses's disobedience and Zipporah's intercession. Zipporah by her blood sacrifice acted as a mediator between God and her family. Once again, the traditions of Zipporah and Huldah taught us that women through intercessory prayers should defend their families, our communities and even those who consider us to be outsiders or enemies. You should be a building pillar and not a destroying caterpillar. These typical exemplary women were called, not because of who their husbands were by status, record or what their husbands did, but because they were available and open to God's calling in their lives.

- **Deborah interceded for Israel** when the Canaanites were oppressing them. Where men failed, Deborah intervened.

- **Hannah interceded** for a child God would use
**Intercession In the New Testament**
- **Paul's Intercession**

Pauls Prayer for the Colossians for knowledge, wisdom and spiritual understanding. - There comes a time in the body of Christ when doctrinal confusion, false teaching and teachers or anti gospel or ungodly government decision arises etc. Only intercession will provide God's intervention.

- **I remember the case of false prophesy of Rev. Jimmy** Jones properly known as James Warren Jones (May 13, 1931 – November 18, 1978), an American preacher that led to hundreds of deaths of ignorant worshippers. Pastor of the Peoples Temple cult church then dreamt of what he called "revolutionary suicide" and orchestrated a mass murder-suicide in Jonestown, Guyana, on November 18, 1978.

- *V.9 It is because of these things that we have not stopped praying for you. We have prayed ever since the day that Epaphras told us news about you. We ask God that his Spirit will cause you to understand things properly. So you will know completely and clearly what God wants you to do* (Col. 1 - EasyEnglishVersion).

- **Importance and strategy of corporate intercession in spiritual warfare** (Ex. 17:11-16)
- **Rom 8:26 NHEB**

*And in the same way, the Spirit also helps us in our weakness, for we do not know how to pray as we ought. But the Spirit himself makes intercession for us with inexpressible groanings.*

- Intercession (*huperentugchanō* ) in the original language means to intercede for one, to intercede on behalf of
- **In Rom. 8:27 (AMP)**

*And He Who searches the hearts of men knows what is in the mind of the [Holy] Spirit [what His intent is], because the Spirit intercedes and pleads [before God] in behalf of the saints according to and in harmony with God's will.*

- In verse 27 Intercession (entugchanō ) denotes to entreat (in favor or against), meet someone for the purpose of conversation, consultation, or supplication.

- It is the Messiah Jesus who is interceding on our behalf... is seated at the right hand of God (v. 34 ISV)

- Still referring to the continuous or incomplete work of Christ here.

Therefore, He is able also to save to the uttermost (completely, perfectly, finally, and for all time and eternity) those who come to God through Him, since He is always living to make petition to God and intercede with Him and intervene for them (Heb. 7:25 AMP).

**- Further studies:**

1Tim 2:1, 2 Corinthians 1:11, Philippians 1:19, Nehemiah 1: 4-11, Isaiah 62:6-7, Genesis 24:12-14, Rom. 10:1, James 5:14, Matt. 5:44,

## Numbers 12:13 (AMP)

*And Moses cried to the Lord, saying, heal her now, O God, I beseech You!*

- Acts 7:60, Luke 22:32, 23:34, Matt. 18:19,20; Philemon 1:22

**- The Disciples interceded** for a replacement of Judas who by transgression fell from the grace and his bishoprick and apostleship another must take (Acts 1:24 - 25).

**- Paul and associates interceded for the new converts in Christ**.

*9. For this reason we also, from the day we heard of it, have not ceased to pray and make [special] request for you, [asking] that you may be filled with the full (deep and clear) knowledge of His will in all spiritual wisdom [in comprehensive insight into the ways and purposes of God] and in understanding and discernment of spiritual things—*

*10. That you may walk (live and conduct yourselves) in a manner worthy of the Lord, fully pleasing to Him and desiring to please Him in all things, bearing fruit in every good work and steadily growing and increasing in and by the knowledge of God [with fuller, deeper, and clearer insight, acquaintance, and recognition].*

11. [We pray] that you may be invigorated and strengthened with all power according to the might of His glory, [to exercise] every kind of endurance and patience (perseverance and forbearance) with joy,

12. Giving thanks to the Father, who has qualified and made us fit to share the portion which is the inheritance of the saints (Gods holy people) in the Light (Colossians 1:9-12, AMP).

- Paul prays for the Christians at Ephesus to be strong

**14 For this reason, then, I bend my knees to pray to the** Father (Ephesians 3:14-19)

- Paul prays for the believers at Thessalonica for Encouragement in Persecution

2 Thess 1:11

Wherefore also we pray always for you, that our God would count you worthy of this calling, and fulfil all the good pleasure of his goodness, and the work of faith with power:

- "In life's journey it is better to be a supporting pillar than a destroying caterpillar"

****

- Unction cannot be learned but can be earned by prayers. Victory is not in the pulpit but in the prayer closet - Leanard Ravenhill


- But you beloved, building up your most holy faith, PRAYING IN THE HOLY GHOST - Jude


- Prayer was pre-eminently the business of his life - Edwin Payson biography


- whole days and weeks have I spent prostrate on the ground in silence or vocal prayers - George Whitefield

# 3 CONTEMPORARY INTERCESSORS

- **Most of the people opposed** to a particular military junta regime were eliminated clandestinely including pastors in my country. An occasion I bought an evening news paper, ran to one of our brothers almost in tears and screamed, "why are they killing our prophets?" I handed the papers to him about a Bishop who was close to him that was shot. One of the visiting ministers in a convention shared how when they were approaching our air space, he saw a very big woman incubating the whole air space over our country. This huge woman occupying the air space was said to be the principality controlling the polity and economy of our country. It is only in spiritual warfare, strategic spiritual warfare can this type of national principality be overthrown and dethroned. They are all intruders.

- In contemporary times, there are many well-known intercessors, such as praying Hyde, George Muller, David Brainerd, Payson, Rees Howells, who founded the Bible College of Wales and had a powerful intercessory ministry.

- **John Nelson Hyde:**
They called him praying Hyde, the Apostle of prayer, the man who never sleeps because of his life style. It all began when the dream, hunger, the passion, the burden of a devout Presbyterian pastor rubbed off on the children. Just like

when a disciple of Christ watched Jesus pray in Luke 11:1, something ignited in him and he poured out his soul and requested, "Lord teach us to pray." Not even how to pray but to pray. That was what happened to the Hyde's family. They heard their father intercede for God to send laborers into the harvest field. John's senior brother Edmund caught the vision but died midway so John carried the vision and studied to go to the mission field in Punjab, India. Despite the persecutions, his handicaps, few converts, he never lost the vision. Most time hes withdrawn studying his bible. He invited other missionaries to join him to intercede for spiritual breakthroughs. In fact, in 1899, his passion for souls increased so much that drove him whole nights on his face before God. John's letter below, to his college revealed his burden:

"Have felt led to pray for others this winter as never before. I never before knew what it was to work all day and then pray all night before God for another. In college or at parties at home, I used to keep such hours for myself, or pleasure, and can I not do as much for God and souls?"

- it is only passion or burden for the lost soul which the holy spirit gives to the hungry will sustain this move. May God send us intercessors to build up the hedge and stand in the gap.

- John Hyde in 1904 led some Indian converts and some American missionaries into the first Punjab Prayer Union convention at Pakistan where each person set aside time to pray for revival. The Holy Spirit and the anointing fell on them all. Every year they gather to fast and pray for revival and salvation of lost souls. Hyde's vision, discernment of spirits, and burden for souls was astounding. In 1908 he was led to pray for the salvation of one Indian every day and the result was great that 365 souls converted to Christ that year. Then he started praying for two souls every day and about 800 converts were recorded that year. Give me souls, God, or I die! showed the weight of the burden on his soul for a lost world. John denied himself food, sleep, pleasure just to fulfill his ministry and call of God on his life.

- John Hyde witnessed a wave of great revival sweep through India and the Punjab.

- He wrote before he died:

*"On the day of prayer, God gave me a new experience. I seemed to be away above our conflict here in the Punjab and I saw God's great battle in all India, and then away out beyond in China, Japan, and Africa. I saw how we had been thinking in narrow circles of our own countries and in our own denominations, and how God was now rapidly joining force to force and line to line, and all was beginning to be one great struggle. That, to me, means the great triumph of Christ. We must exercise the greatest care to be utterly obedient to Him who sees all the battlefield all the time. It is only He who can put each man in the place where his life can count for the most."*

Steve Porter said of John Hyde:

"In the end, he spent countless dark nights, praying and weeping on the cold, bare floor, not sleeping or eating, interceding for souls, which came first, one a day, then two a day, until four and then eight souls were saved each day and baptized into the kingdom. The burden to pray was so heavy that it could be felt by those who were nearby, who were similarly affected. Hydess bed was rarely slept in, because he spent most nights groaning for souls on the floor, and as a result, the number of converts all over India grew by leaps and bounds.

### - David Brainerd:

Brainerd was born in 1718. He lived for 29 years, eight of which he did as a Christian. Though he suffered disease attacks and tuberculosis yet Brainerd did exploits for the kingdom on bended kneels.

**Read from David's Diary**: *(Notes from The Life and Diary of David Brainerd by Jonathan Edwards).*

- As a missionary to the Indians Brainerd's life strongly impacted the lives of many. Jonathan Edwards preserved and edited his diaries and published it with special notes in

1749 as The Life and Diary of David Brainerd. His biography has been a great challenge and encouragement to the body of Christ. See what the people said about his life:

Let every preacher read carefully over the Life of Brainerd - John Wesley

Perusing the life of David Brainerd, his soul was filled with a holy emulation of that extraordinary man; and after deep consideration and fervent prayer, he was at length fixed in a resolution to imitate his example - Henry Martyn"

"Edwards publication of Life of Brainerd is a sacred text - **William Carey"**

Satan trembles when he sees the weakest saint upon his knees - William Cowper"

"Brainerds heart of prayer and intercession moved me. I, like so many before me who have read his entries, wanted to emulate him. He never gave up investing hours on his knees crying out in prayer - Jonathan Edward"

- Brainerd struggled with chronic sickness, depression, and loneliness under harsh living conditions as a missionary. He was upon his knees despite his condition and God so much saw him through.

- Brainerd was a praying and fasting believer. He talked of praying the whole day and fasting was a lifestyle.

Brainerd wrote, "God has been pleased to keep my soul hungry, almost continually... I feel my desires of him the more insatiable, and my thirsting after holiness the more unquenchable

- Extract from David Brainerd's Diary:

Ten Diary Entries on Fasting and Prayer

- Monday, April 19. I set apart this day for fasting, and prayed to God for his grace; specially to prepare me for the work of the ministry, to give me divine aid and direction in my preparations for that great work, and in his own time to send me into his harvest. Accordingly, in the morning, I endeavored to plead for the divine presence for the day, and not without some life. In the forenoon, I felt the power of intercession for precious, immortal souls; for the advancement of the kingdom of my dear Lord and Savior in the word; and withal, a most sweet resignation, and even consolation and joy in the thoughts of suffering hardships, distresses, and even death itself, in the promotion of it; and had special enlargement in pleading for the enlightening and conversion of the poor heathen. In the afternoon, God was with me of a truth. O it was blessed company indeed! God enabled me so to agonize in prayer, that I was quite wet with perspiration, though in the shade, and the cool wind. My soul was drawn out very much for the world; for multitudes of souls. I think I had more enlargement for sinners, than for the children of God; though I felt as if I could spend my life in cries for both. I enjoyed great sweetness in communion with my dear Savior. I think I never in my life felt such an entire weanedness from this world, and so much resigned to God in everything. O that I may always live to and upon my blessed God! Amen, Amen.

- Monday, May 3. ... In the morning I withdrew to my usual place of retirement, and mourned for my abuse of my dear Lord: spent the day in fasting and prayer. God gave me much power of wrestling for his cause and kingdom; and it was a happy day to my soul...

- Monday, June 14. .. I set apart this day for secret fasting and prayer, to entreat God to direct and bless me with regard to the great work... God enabled me to wrestle ardently in intercession for absent friends: but just at night, the Lord visited me marvelously in prayer... I wrestled for absent friends, for the ingathering of souls, for multitudes of poor souls, and for many that I thought were the children of God, personally, in many distant places. I was in such an agony, from sun half an hour high, till near dark, that I was all over wet with sweat; but yet it seemed to me that I had wasted away the day, and had done nothing. Oh, my dear Jesus did sweat blood for poor souls! I longed for more compassion towards them

- Wednesday, April 20. Set apart this day for fasting and prayer, to bow my soul before God for the bestowment of divine grace; especially that all my spiritual afflictions and inward distresses might be sanctified to my soul... I spent the day in the woods alone, and there poured out my complaint to God. O that God would enable me to live to his glory for the future!

- Thursday, Nov. 3. Spent this day in secret fasting and prayer, from morning till night. My soul was ardent in prayer, was enabled to wrestle ardently for myself, for Christian friends, and for the church of God. And felt more desire to see the power of God in the conversion of souls, than I have done for a long season. Blessed be God for this season of fasting and prayer! May his goodness always abide with me, and draw my soul to him!

- Thursday, Dec. 22. Spent this day alone in fasting and prayer, and reading in Gods word the exercises and deliverances of his children... O that Zion might become the joy of the whole earth! It is better to wait upon God with patience, than to put confidence in anything in this lower world. My soul, wait thou on the Lord; for from him comes thy salvation.

- Tuesday, Jan. 3... When I return home, and give myself to meditation, prayer, and fasting, a new scene opens to my mind, and my soul longs for mortification, self-denial, humility, and divorcement from all the things of the world. This evening my heart was somewhat warm and fervent in prayer and meditation, so that I was loth to indulge sleep. Continued in those duties till about midnight.

- Friday, Jan. 6. Feeling and considering my extreme weakness, and want of grace, the pollution of my soul, and danger of temptations on every side, I set apart this day for fasting and prayer, neither eating nor drinking from evening to evening, beseeching God to have mercy on me. My soul intensely longed, that the dreadful spots and stains of sin might be washed away from it. Saw something of the power and all-sufficiency of God. My soul seemed to rest on his power and grace; longed for resignation to his will, and mortification to all things here below. My mind was greatly fixed on divine things: my resolutions for a life of mortification, continual watchfulness, self-denial, seriousness, and devotion, were strong and fixed; my desires ardent and intense; my conscience tender, and afraid of every appearance of evil.

- Thursday. Dec. 6. I set apart this day for secret prayer and fasting, to implore the blessing of God on myself, on my poor people, on my friends, and on the church of God.

- Note: Note the secrecy of his dealings with God. Not like the Pharisees and Sadducees who show off their deeds to receive glory from man. When we fast in secret, our God who sees and knows the secret of the hearts of men will reward us accordingly. Maybe only group fast can be announced publicly to those concerned. Note also the nature of his intercession for others.

**- George Muller:**

George Muller was one of the worlds mightiest intercessors. A mighty prayer warrior George Muller, would spend the majority of his life caring for the orphans in Bristol, England. On March 10th, 1898, George was found lying on the floor beside his bed! Heaven had welcomed another mighty prayer warrior. People would come from all over the world to pay their respects. Thousands lined the streets to remember the man who fed orphans for over fifty years through the POWER of PRAYER! Hear him:

*"Neither eloquence nor depth of thought makes a truly great preacher. Only a life of prayer and meditation will render him a vessel ready for the Master's use and fit to be employed in the conversion of sinners and in the edification of the saints."*

On October 7, 1830, I was united in marriage to Miss Mary Groves. This step was taken after much prayer and from a full conviction that it was better for me to be married. I have never regretted either the step itself or the choice, but I am truly grateful to God for giving me such a wife.

- When God gives a spirit of prayer, it is easy to pray! I spent about three hours in prayer over Psalms 64 and 65. In reference to that precious word, "0 thou that hearest prayer" (Psa. 65:2), I asked the Lord the following petitions and entreated Him to record them in heaven and to answer them: That He would give me grace to glorify Him by a submissive and patient spirit under my affliction.

- January 3, 1842. This evening we had a precious prayer meeting. When the usual time for closing the meeting came, some of us wanted to continue to wait upon the Lord. I suggested that those who had bodily strength, time, and a desire to wait longer upon the Lord, do so. At least thirty remained, and we continued in prayer until after ten. I never knew deeper prayer in the Spirit. I experienced an unusual nearness to the Lord and was able to pray in faith, without doubting.

- January 4. The Lord has answered all our requests concerning the daily needs of the orphans. We have had an abundance these last several days, but the expenses have been great also."

- Muller interceded for more than fifty years for the salvation of a small group of men. Learn from the patience of Muller if you are weary of long delayed or unanswered prayers. Evangelist George Muller worked with orphans in Bristol, England and through his intercessory prayers experienced God's great provisions for his orphanage in the 19th-century. Muller is best known for the large faith-based orphan ministry he carried out in Bristol, England, in the nineteenth century. He was also a diligent, disciplined man of prayer. He kept an ongoing prayer notebook in which he recorded his requests on one page and the answer to each of those petitions on the facing page. By this means he persevered in praying till he received answers to thousands of specific requests.

Once while ministering in Dusseldorf, Germany, Muller was approached by a missionary to that city who was distressed because his six sons remained unconverted, though he had been praying for them many years. He encouraged the missionary to continue in prayers and expect results.

Six years later, when they met again the happy results were that two months after Muller had left five of the man's sons had come to faith in Christ and the sixth on his way to embracing the faith.

### - Watchman Nee:

Nee spent most of his life in communist prison for preaching Christ. Never enjoyed his marriage being separated from his wife. The evil government used his brains in translations of books into their native language and into English. The prison walls never stopped him. Who had written great Christian books with divine insight than this man of God or would I say Man from God or both. Are you a Man of God or a Man sent from God - an emissary or both.

### - Rees Howells:

During World War 11 arose a Welsh who lived a life of Intercession for souls and profound prayer Life. Rees Howells, also ran and founded a Bible College in Wales. Rees Howells story was said to be a life lived for God. In 1921 a group accountant of the National Coal Board, by name Mr. Henry Griffiths, gave an account of his personal experience with Howells. He wrote:

"I read about the mighty movement of the Spirit through him in Africa. He was coming to Lanelly, so I walked three miles to hear him. He was to me the most wonderful missionary I had read of. His way of speaking was different, the Spirit had so dealt with him. I remember one young Christian asking him how he knew Gods voice, and he said, Cant you tell your mothers voice from any other? Yes, of course, the young man answered. Well, I know His voice just like that. I shall never forget the meetings in the Llandrindod Convention after he came back from Africa. Frankly, he was by himself. He was only about forty years old and in the strength of his manhood. He lifted the meeting to such a plane that everyone was spellbound. No one could move, no one could follow him. He was requested to test the meeting and asked who would like to give themselves to God as he had done, and everyone stood up, ministers and all. At ministers meeting the next day, to which I was allowed to come, Mr. Paget Wilkes was speaking. He was quick enough to recognize the Spirit in Mr. Howells, and said, there is someone here among us, and I feel like going round the country with him, carrying his bag and cleaning his boots. May God meet with many in reading this book, as He has met with the author in writing it. *Norman P. Grubb*."

## - Praying Payson

They called him praying Payson. He devoted himself to a disciplined life of prayers and Bible reading when he was convinced of God's call on his life. Payson read Jonathan Edwards books. In continuous prayers his emptiness and sinfulness like Isaiah became real to him. He saw how vile he was.

"Woe is me! for I am undone; because I am a man of unclean lips, and I dwell in the midst of a people of unclean lips: for mine eyes have seen the King, the LORD of hosts (Isa. 6:5)."

Most times Payson lay prostrate with open bible before him, interceding in prayers. In 1807, his work and life earned him a pastoral appointment in Portland, Maine. A peep into his diary read in part

"... *but what was said seemed to come with power. Many were in tears, and all seemed stirred up...*"

Payson was effective in soul-winning, the result of growth in his church. Like many ministers of his time, you must show spiritual fruits as proof of your repentance Unlike what we have today. Payson's letter below to his mother in September of 1809, revealed some truth about his operational method.

"Last Communion, we admitted 11 to the church, and next Sabbath we shall admit 12 more. He went on, the appetite for hearing seems insatiable, and our assemblies are more crowded than ever..."

During the 20 years of his ministry, his church was said to

have received more than 700 new converts. His diary revealed the secret of this success to be intercession. He wrote at 26 "... Was enabled to agonize in prayer for myself and [my] people, and to make intercession with unutterable groanings. " He was nicknamed Praying Payson and it had been said that the wooden floor at his bedside was worn by his knees. He preached with passion

- We must learn from Edward Payson the experiential knowledge of power with God which he exuded by spending much time in prayers and Bible study. Payson's humility enhanced his relationship with God. God's power was safe in his hands (2 Corinthians 13:4).

"In all my conversation with this wonderful man (Edward Payson), I never heard him utter a word that bordered on boasting, or savored of pride but he seemed to have a surprising sense of his own unworthiness, and of the amazing love of God in making himself known to him. And giving him a hope in his mercy - A fellow minister"

- We must learn to pray and intercede for others from him for therein is his success

- Charles Simeon, a contemporary of Payson, said every minister must learn three things from Payson - 1. humility 2. humility and 3. humility.

-Andrew Murray:

Andrew Murray was a South African minister and writer. He wrote and taught a great deal on the importance of intercessory prayers in the life of a Christian.

- Andrew Murray's Sample of 31 days Help Guide for Effective Intercession: Murray gave a 31 days sample of what to pray and how to pray them citing related and relevant scriptures for each day with some explanations. Let see sample of day two and three of his guide below.

DAY TWO

WHAT TO PRAY:For the Spirit of Supplication

Scriptures: The Spirit himself intercedes for us Romans 8:26

I will pour out a spirit of supplication Zechariah 12:10

HOW TO PRAY In the Spirit

Pray at all times in the Spirit, with all prayer and supplication. Eph. 6:18 pray in the Holy Spirit; Jude 20

- DAY THREE

WHAT TO PRAY: For all Christians

Scriptures: Pray at all times in the Spirit with all prayer and supplication. To that end keep alert with all perseverance, making supplication for all the Christians,

Ephesians 6:18 Every member of a body is interested in the welfare of the whole, and exists to help and complete the others.

HOW TO PRAY In the Love of the Spirit

By this all people will know that you are my disciples, if you have love for one another. John 13:35

I pray that they may all be one; so that the world may believe that thou hast sent me. John 17:21

I appeal to you, brethren, by our Lord Jesus Christ and by the love of the Spirit, to strive together with me in your prayers to God on my behalf, Romans 15:30

Above all hold unfailing your love for one another, 1 Peter 4:8

- You can write and plan out your own guide as the spirit of God leads in your own situation and environment. As a child of God who has the spirit of God never copy other people's brain but you can learn from them. Wait on God to give you message tailored to the needs of your audience and congregation. Stop turning the internet as your holy spirit. Only lazy ministers do that. God can teach you from the life of others.

- William Carey

William Carey called the father of modern mission. fought and stopped the cultural practices of suttee (in which a widow was burned alive with the body of her husband) and infanticide in India. He established a college and translated the Bible into Indian dialects. But back home in England, William Carey shared his pains and work with a bedridden and almost paralyzed sister, Polly. Polly in her condition for

52 years interceded for the missionary needs of her brother, William Carey. The story of praying Polly should challenge the handicapped, the sick or old believers. You can pray for them, if you cannot go. We sing,

"Let the Lord send me. When the Lord needed somebody, let the Lord send me." He's sending our kneeling knees. Kneeling we triumph.

- Young Missionary with the China Inland Mission. He ventured into a village dreaded by other missionaries. Bandits there would kill any stranger or foreigner that visit them. This young missionary was warned not to go but the burden to win soul drove him to damn the consequences. He came back successfully to the surprise of other missionaries and shared testimonies to the church back home in England. How the bandits rumored that he escaped because of the eleven body guard soldiers that followed him. They were surprised because he went alone. They then knew that God had sent his angels to protect him. He never saw those angels but the villagers and bandits saw them. What was the secret of his success? Back home the church had gathered few days before his dangerous journey to intercede for him. Only 11 persons responded to the pastor's call for volunteer intercessors. The pastor was disappointed at the number. However they prayed. Is there any relationship in numbers to the 11 that prayed and the 11 soldiers that accompanied the young preacher. Many are called but few are chosen. Dare to challenge God?

**- This reminds me of an encounter our church** had with the state government that would warrant pulling down the church building for road obstruction. Humanly speaking surveys showed that the church was on the middle of that road. We had none to stand for us but God. The leaders called for prayer and fasting. Out of a church of hundreds not up to 10 persons responded. But during that occasion I was leading. As I led in prayers at the end, we said amen. I heard more voices said amen. I was happy more people have joined but when we got up no new persons came in while we were praying. Where did the extra voices came from. However, I knew God had answered our prayers. Is over 30 years now, that road was diverted because of the church. God sent his angels to chorus amen with the few of us there. Just because some people gathered and interceded for the whole day for God's intervention in the affairs of men, God answered his people in that African church.

****

- No man is greater than his prayer life. The pastor who is not praying is playing. The people who are not praying are straying - Leonard Ravenhill

- I sought for a man - Ezekiel 22:30

- Elias was a man - James 5:17

- As soon as we cease to bleed, we cease to bless - Dr. J H Jowett

# 4 INTERCESSION AND SPIRITUAL WARFARE

- **I visited a relation in a place distant** from where I lived. They said thank God you came. What is the matter? This woman had been pregnant for about three or more years (beyond gestation period of nine months). This is what we call locked up pregnancy. She accused the mother-in-law of locking up her womb and the mother-in -law is now dead. She said God put in the child there. Yes, but it is not God that delayed the delivery. Sometimes you find out that the child is talking inside there or when delivered had developed teeth. Strange but real. What do you do? Intercession and spiritual warfare. You first deal with forces that spiritually locked up the womb before attending to the captive.

- **Spiritual warfare** is a battle we fight with our spirit in the spiritual realm against spiritual forces of darkness. So, it is not our battle but the Lord's. Then to succeed we need spiritual discernment, and being sensitive to the leading of the spirit. Know God's will, have faith in God. In spiritual warfare we need continuous prayers in season and out of season. Be alert and vigilant for the enemy is roaming about seeking for a loophole.

- **Intercession is an important weapon of warfare**. To be successful you must Know your enemy (Satan) and acknowledge your spiritual strength and who you are in Christ. In the physical war if you know the capacity, the size of the enemy's army and weaponry, then you can plot for their downfall. Have you not seen where the super powers have been defeated by a lesser army. Even where the lesser power who knew the scene of battle thoroughly captures the sophisticated weapon of the enemy and use it to fight back. So, in spiritual warfare. So, in intercession we know the devices of the enemy. We know who we are up against and we know who we are too. The devil might be mighty but mightier and greater is He that is in us.

... for we are not ignorant of his devices (2Co 2:11)

We know his strategies, tricks and cunning devices. Every intercessor must know the battle strategies and strongholds of the enemy before you can plunder him and set his captives free.

Or else how can one enter into a strong man's house, and spoil his goods, except he first binds the strong man? and then he will spoil his house (Mat 12:29 KJV).

- Bind (*deō* ) denotes to put in chains, into bondage before you can release his captives.

... ought not this woman, a daughter of Abraham, whom Satan has kept bound for eighteen years, be loosed from this bond?

### Eph 6:12-13 (Easy English)

*12.You need to be strong because we are not fighting against human enemies. No, but instead we are fighting against the rulers and the powerful spirits that have authority over this dark world. We are fighting against powerful bad spirits who live in the heavens.*

*13 So, take the whole armor that God gives. Then you will be able to stand against the enemy when he attacks. And he will not be able to move you from your place. Then, after you have done everything, you will still be standing strongly in your place.*

### - Intercessor you are up against:

- *principalities (authorities, rulers)*

- *powers (powerful spirits that have authority over this dark world*
- *rulers of the darkness of this world (cosmic powers in the darkness around us, the world rulers of this darkness)*
- *spiritual wickedness in high places (powerful bad spirits who live in the heavens, evil spiritual forces in the heavenly realm).*
- But God has given us armors, whole, full, complete, suitable weapons, spiritual missiles the enemy will not withstand.
- **Whole** (Gr. *panoplia* = full armor, complete armor includes shield, sword, lance, helmet, greaves, and breastplate). Never go to war with incomplete or depleted armor. Remember all the armors are for the front. None for the back side. And Jesus said unto him, no man, having put his hand to the plough, and looking back, is fit for the kingdom of God. Backsliders are not for this kind of war.

*So, if a man therefore purge himself, he shall be a vessel unto honor, sanctified, and meet for the master's use, and prepared unto every good work.*

-To save others we must save ourselves first. Also, in trying to save others we grow into fortifying ourselves in the Lord. Purity of life and holiness is important in this our journey.

- Yes, this is fearful and worrisome. For 18yrs. The devil is wicked but God is merciful. Through intercessory prayers we break down stronghold, upturn wicked judgement decreed, destroy satanic covens. Yes, remember we are not fighting for victory but from victory already secured by Christ death on the cross. Christ has given us authority, delegated power, (Gr. exousia meaning power of choice, privilege, influence, permission, the power of him whose will and commands must be submitted to by others and obeyed).

- Beloved God has given you authority to overrule the enemy and set the captives free - whether

**lawful captives**
**Secret Captives**

**Open Captives**
**Partial Captives or**
**Total Captives**

and the prey of the enemy (For more see my book on Strategic Spiritual Warfare)

Luke 10:19 KJV

Behold, I give unto you power to tread on serpents and scorpions, and over all the power of the enemy: and nothing shall by any means hurt you.

- Amplified version of the Bible put it's this way:

Behold! I have given you authority and power to trample upon serpents and scorpions, and [physical and mental strength and ability] over all the power that the enemy [possesses]; and nothing shall in any way harm you.

**- Intercession with fasting, praise and worship** will intensify and boost our intercession and help sensitize or energize our spirit. It is an armor too. Daniel never confronted these principalities on full hungry food. He prayed, he fasted for 21 full days. Desperate situations need desperate remedies and attentions (Daniel 10:12-13).

*(For more on fasting see my book on fasting, "Fasting: Experiencing God's Power and Breaking Spiritual Barriers)*

**2Cor. 10:3-5**

For though we walk in the flesh, we do not war after the flesh: (For the weapons of our warfare are not carnal, but mighty through God to the pulling down of strong holds;). Casting down imaginations, and every high thing that exalteth itself against the knowledge of God, and bringing into captivity every thought to the obedience of Christ;

**- Eph 6:10-12**

*Finally, my brethren, be strong in the Lord, and in the power of his might. 11 Put on the whole armor of God, that ye may be able to stand against the wiles of the devil. 12 For we wrestle not against flesh and blood, but against principalities, against powers, against the rulers of the darkness of this world, against spiritual wickedness in high places.*

1Jn 5:19 KJV And we know that we are of God, and the whole world lieth in wickedness.

**- Intercession in warfare scriptures:**

- ... it occurred that He (Jesus) went up into a mountain to pray, and spent the whole night in prayer to God. And when it was day, He summoned His disciples and selected from them twelve, whom He named apostles (special messengers) - Luke 6:12-13 AMP.

- The soldiers of Manasseh, Reuben and Gad believed God. They prayed to God while they fought. So God helped them. So, they won the war against the Hagrites and against all the other people who were helping the Hagrites.

(1 Chronicles 5:20 EasyEnglish)

**...Watch and pray** ...the spirit indeed is willing, but the flesh is weak. " (Matthew 26:41 NKJV)

...men always ought to pray and not to faint (Luke 18:1-14)

**... be serious and watchful in your prayers**. (1 Peter 4:7)

**... pray without ceasing**... (1 Thessalonians 5:16-18)

**... Praying always with all** prayer and supplication in the Spirit, and watching thereunto with all perseverance and supplication for all saints;

(Ephesians 6:18)

**- Pray for the peace of Jerusalem**: ... (Psalm 122:6)

**- These all continued with one accord in prayer** and supplication, with the women and Mary the mother of Jesus, and with His brothers. (Acts 1:14)

****

- The narrow way is still narrow and God has no intention of expanding it to accommodate your new found ungodly appendages.


- War in the spirit is not for those who are children in understanding, novice in skill or shallow in knowledge. The sons of Sceva were victims of Ignorance.


- There is no victory without a war. There is no prize without a price.


- There is no crown without a cross. There is no crown of glory without a crown of thorns. Pleasure is just the other side of pain.

# 5 JESUS CHRIST OUR INTERCESSOR:

### Rom. 8:34 (AMP,)
*Who is there to condemn [us]? Will Christ Jesus (the Messiah), Who died, or rather Who was raised from the dead, who is at the right hand of God actually pleading as He intercedes for us?*

- **Right hand, right side** (Gr. *dexios*) of God here denotes metaphorically a place of honor or authority where he sits and intercede for the saints.

### - Heb. 7:25 (AMP)
Therefore, He is able also to save to the uttermost (completely, perfectly, finally, and for all time and eternity) those who come to God through Him, since He is always living to make petition to God and intercede with Him and intervene for them.

- How powerful intercession is

ISV version put it such:

*25 Therefore, because he always lives to intercede for them, he is able to save completely those who come to God through him.*

*26 We need such a high priest one who is holy, innocent, pure, set apart from sinners, exalted above the heavens.*

- **Jesus Prays for Himself, His Disciples, and His**

## Future Followers
### John 17:19 - 20

19 And for their sakes I sanctify myself, that they also might be sanctified through the truth.

20 Neither pray I for these alone, but for them also which shall believe on me through their word

### - Isa 53:12

*So, I will give many peoples to him. And he will have the strong people as his gift. These are the reasons. He poured out his life until he died. He let people count him in with bad people. Also, he carried the sin of many people. And he prayed for the people who had not obeyed Gods rules (EasyEnglish)*

**- Intercession is Jesus' high priestly function**, whereby he takes the weakness of the people upon himself and stands in their stead to make pleas for the people. Romans 8:34 and Acts 7:55 of Stephen's vision conformed the positional standing of Christ.

*"But Stephen, filled with the Holy Spirit, looked straight into heaven and saw the glory of God and Jesus standing at the right hand of God - Act 7:55 ISV)"*

**- Christ is interceding for us.**

**Further Reading:**

1 Jon 2:1 (...we have an advocate [intercessor] with the Father, Jesus Christ the righteous)

Luke 6:12 (that he [Jesus] went out into a mountain to pray, and continued all night in prayer to God), Matt. 14:22-33

**- Watchman Intercessor**

Watchman what of the night?

*... Watchman, what of the night? Watchman, what of the night? Isa. 21:11*

**- Watchman** (*shaˆ mar*) denotes properly to hedge about (as with thorns), guard; generally, to protect, to keep, observe, give heed, have charge of, wait for, keep watch and ward, save life.

**- Watchman intercessor is a Gatekeepers** (security)

at the gate, the entrance to the city and people
- *Watchman must see, spy out (intelligence report):*
- *Watchman must hear from God:*
- *Watchman must proclaim publish and warn the people of impending danger.* The voice of the people before God and man
- **Watchman intercessor is guard and protector.**

\*\*\*\*

- There is no call without a cost. An altar without a heaven accepted sacrifice is an altar without a heaven -sent fire.

- Ordinary Men with Extraordinary Power. Common Men with Uncommon Results. Usual Men with Unusual Anointing. Weak Men with Mighty Deeds are born out of the closet experience.

- Don't wait indefinitely for open doors to come, create one yourself or you may die of old age waiting.

- God will use the Simplicity in man to establish the complexity of God,

- You can create success out of failure. You can create gain out of loss. You can create abundance out of lack. You can create promotion out of demotion. You can create advantage out of disadvantage.
- Rise above the storm. Be above and not under the

circumstances.

# 6 ACTIVE ELEMENTS OF INTERCESSION

- I remember a time after we finished a crusade I couldn't go home with others. I couldn't sleep. A heavy load sort of was laid on me to pray for the converts. No word was coming but heavy groaning and travail all through the night. Then in the morning I received the Holy Spirit baptism and it became somehow difficult praying in ordinary language from that day. Burden brings groaning and travail. Travail leads to birth. Prayer burden is one of the active elements of intercession *(for more see my book, "Strategic Spiritual Warfare").*

- **Consecration** is from the root word (Heb. qâ dash) meaning to consecrate, dedicate, be holy, be sanctified, be separate, to be set apart, be treated as sacred, devote or (Gr. hagiazo) denoting to separate from profane things and dedicate to God, dedicate to God, to purify, to cleanse externally, to purify by expiation: free from the guilt of sin, to purify internally by renewing of the soul

- *And so, for their sake and on their behalf, I sanctify (dedicate, consecrate) Myself, that they also may be sanctified (dedicated, consecrated, made holy) in the Truth. (John 17:19 AMP)*

## Ephesians 6 18

"With every prayer and request, pray at all times in

43

the Spirit, and stay alert in this, with all perseverance and intercession for all the saints"

**Romans 8:26 NIV**

*In the same way, the Spirit helps us in our weakness. We do not know what we ought to pray for, but the Spirit himself intercedes for us through wordless groans.*

**John 17:19 (AMP)**

*And so, for their sake and on their behalf, I sanctify (dedicate, consecrate) Myself, that they also may be sanctified (dedicated, consecrated, made holy) in the Truth.*

- Anyone who must take up this task or calling or ministry of intercession must consecrate himself or herself. An intercessor must set himself or herself apart in living a holy life or he will experience the fall of the sons of Sceva who wanted to cast out demons with a religious formula. "Paul, I know, Jesus I know but who are you?"

**I remember the case of a brother**, so called then involved in occult and still wanted the gift of the holy spirit, at the same time. It cannot work. You cannot serve God and Mammon. We went to evangelism together but he ran mental at that camp meeting. Or the case of a brother who loved the work of God. He went and laid hands on a demon possessed and demons transferred from this man into him because he's not properly armed and prepared. Every intercessor's and by extension every believer's private life who is involved in spiritual warfare must pass through the crucible. Purity and holy living must be part of your life so the enemy, your profession, confession and God will not find you wanting.

**- Groaning in prayers:**

Groaning is a low, mournful sound uttered in pain or grief, uttered in frustration, disapproval, emanating from applied pressure or weight. Such prayers come from burden deposited by the holy spirit. You remember Jesus prayers in Mar 14:36

*He said, Abba, (my Father), you can do anything. Please take this pain away from me. But I do not ask you to do what*

*I want. I choose what you want (Easy English Version).*

- You can feel the weight behind that utterance. Groaning can take you long in prayers. There are many times in prayers I have found myself interceding in prayers nonstop for six or more hours. When the spirit of intercessions come on you, continue until the burden lifts. That is when you have peace in your heart.

**- Compassion:**

The dictionary defined compassion as deep awareness of the suffering of another, coupled with the wish to relieve it. This definition fits the life of Christ.

**Mark 6:34**

And Jesus, when he came out, saw much people, and was moved with compassion toward them, because they were as sheep not having a shepherd: and he began to teach them many things.

**Mark 8:2**

*I have compassion on the multitude, because they have now been with me three days, and have nothing to eat:*

**- Prayer Burden:**

Someone defined prayer burden as a load of care or sorrow. It is better experienced than described. It is just like you are bearing willingly a heavy weight, concern, love, godly sorrow about someone in need or something you do that will not let you sleep or eat and sometimes bring you to tears untill you see such a problem solved. Jesus experienced such burden in Gethsemane as recorded in Matthew 26:37-38

*V. 37 And he took with him Peter and the two sons of Zebedee, and became sad and very troubled.*

*V.38 Then says he to them, my soul is very sad, even to death: keep watch with me here.*

- Like Jesus here, sometimes you find someone under this burden fall on his or her face or prostrate in intense spiritual pains. John Elliot, the first to translate the scriptures into a heathen tongue for missionary purposes said among the early Pilgrim Fathers to New England that Prayer and pains, with faith in God can accomplish anything.

- **A sister was washing** and the burden came on her to pray. She stopped and went into prayers noting the time. After sometime, when she felt released, she stopped. The husband came back and said that on the highway he had been sleeping while driving for quite some time (about same time the wife was praying) until the vehicle swerved into the bush and came out. His eyes opened and there was no on-coming vehicle. What I am saying is different from an inner Holy Spirit urge, witness or check. I read about a local brother who prayed for about 24 hours non-stop. It is only burden for souls that will drive you such far where nothing matters, not food, not even time, etc.

- **Prayer Language:**

We were praying for a sister who had an evil covenant with marine spirits. As we started praying in the Spirit, the evil spirit burst into strange tongues with a high pitch. This is a lady I have not known to pray in tongues before. As we cast them out, they confessed to how the mother of this sister in childhood dedicated or initiated her in a particular river. The mother later confirmed it. Outside counterfeit there is the real. We need to pray in the spirit with our prayer language. It terrifies and confuses demons. Intercession grows and thrives more when done in the holy spirit language. Who else knows the will of God? Who else can decipher the heart of man and the mind of the Spirit if not the Holy Spirit?

*... the Spirit also helps us in our weakness, since we do not know how to pray as we should. But the Spirit himself intercedes for us with groans too deep for words ...and the one who searches our hearts knows the mind of the Spirit, for the Spirit intercedes for the saints according to Gods will (Romans 8:26 -27 - ISV).*

In 1Co 14:39B, it says forbid not to speak with tongues, ... do not stop someone when they speak in a special language (EasyEnglish), but let no one be stopped from using tongues (BBE).

- **Intercessory Spirit**: There is a Spirit of intercession, a

Spirit of prayers. For every intercessor, sometimes when you find yourself spiritually dry or you lost your tears and no compassion, you can ask God to restore this intercessory spirit. If during evangelism, you notice an obstacle or a need, the Spirit will ignite the burden in you that you would not care about anything that can keep you from praying. It is praying in the Holy Spirit plus. There is the ministry of intercession

**- Agape Love (God Kind of love):**

Agape is God's kind of Love for everyone and not Eros (sexual love), or Philia (friendship kind of love), Philautia (selfish love) or Storge (family love). Agape does not discriminate. It includes all and excludes none. Every intercessor then must intercede the mind of God when praying for countries, governments, communities or families.

**- Sacrificial Life:**

A life of an intercessor is a life of sacrifice. Others must count before you count. God or God's Agape gave his only son and Jesus gave his only life. Jesus was a given as a sacrificial lamb. Isa 53:5 recorded that he was wounded for our transgressions, he was bruised for our iniquities: the chastisement of our peace was upon him; and with his stripes we are healed. I think of the martyrs gone for the sake of other people's salvation. Look at the books of the Bible, they were products of or written out of sacrifices, pains, prison sentences or excruciating deaths of people who made sacrifices. Book of Revelation was written when John was exiled to Patmos during a time of persecution.

*"I am John, and, like you, I believe Christ. So, I am like a brother to you. Jesus is our king. And because we are his people, we are having trouble. So, like you, I need to be strong and patient. I was on Patmos Island because I had taught Gods message. I told people what is true about Jesus (Rev 1:9 EasyEnglishVersion).*

- **Patmos Island** was near to Asia and the seven churches. The Romans had sent John to Patmos because they did not like him to teach about Jesus. Patmos was a prison. The Romans would not let John leave Patmos. Was it time to mourn? No, it was time for him to write what we read today as book of Revelation.

**- Self-denials and denial of self:**

Things that normally would be to your comfort or enjoyment you give up if it becomes necessary. Be it food, time, or pleasure but for the intercessor duty calls. Self-denial but denial of self, dents your ego and pride. An intercessor is not his or her own but all to God he/she surrenders.

**- Abiding in the Vine (Fruitfulness).** Any intercessor worth its salt must have a strong tie and relationship with the father.

- *If you live in Me [abide vitally united to Me] and My words remain in you and continue to live in your hearts, ask whatever you will, and it shall be done for you (John 15:7, AMP).*

**- Every intercessor must watch and withstand these three enemies:**

 *the world,*

 *- the flesh and*

 *- the devil* (1 John 2:1516; Ephesians 2:23).

- The enemy within (your flesh, the carnal man), the enemy around (the world vanities), and the arch enemy (the devil).

\*\*\*\*

- The misuse of yesterday is what you are suffering today and any misuse today is coding and programming your tomorrow's woes. Now is time to take sides. What do you have?

- God is not looking for capable hands but for available vessels

- Unavailable ability is available disability

- Have you any days of fasting and prayers? Storm the throne of grace and persevere therein and mercy will come down - John Wesley

# 7 CORPORATE INTERCESSION

- **This lady was having running battles** in her life to the point that her parents got very worried. Now she soon became pregnant for a young man who denied taking responsibility. As we went on the offensive binding and losing, a man and a woman ran out of her. She said of the woman that she had threatened to deal with her and she had told her that she could do nothing. The man and woman have been illegal occupants of her body, manipulating and controlling her. They were the source of the strange behaviors she had put up even as a believer. Praise God who intervened.

- **Corporate or Group Intercession** is Exemplified in the case of war against Amalek to execute God's judgement against them.

- *And so it was, when Moses held up his hand that Israel prevailed; and when he let down his hand, Amalek prevailed (Ex. 17:11).*

- **While Joshua and his army**, engaged on the physical field battle (Ex. 17:9) Moses interceded for the army on the hill with the rod of God, rod of authority in his lifted hands. Aaron and Hur supported the hands of Moses. Intercession is a support ministry too. These three groups were active and related. Anything that affected the one affected the other. Note that this was the first fight Israel undertook. Looking at the life of Joshua from here forward, he grew in this anointing of fighting battles.

*- Moses stood on the hill. "Lord, who may abide in your tabernacle? Who may dwell in your holy hill? He who walks uprightly and works righteousness (Ps. 15:1-2)"*

- **Righteousness and holy living** are important for intercessors and prayer warriors if you must escape the hazards and fallouts of fighting the enemy or setting the captives free.

- **Moses also stood with the rod of God in his hand** (rod of authority). An intercessor must know and execute the authority of the believer. Authority is delegated power.

- **Let me illustrate with husband**-and-wife scenario. At home the man is the head while his police wife while on duty as traffic officer will command the husband to stop. The man must stop because the wife there is acting on the power delegated to her by the government. The wife now in the capacity as a traffic officer has authority (delegated power) and can discipline or charge the man (her husband) if he violated the law. So, the intercessor has the backing of God against the forces of darkness or spiritual enemies. Moses also lifted up the rod of God with his hands Lifted (Ex. 17:9, 11).

**May God help us to lift up holy hands.**

*I desire therefore that men pray everywhere, lifting up holy hands, without wrath or doubting (1 Tim. 2:8).*

- **Moses, Aaron and Hur went to the hill top**. In group intercession and warfare, we need corporate anointing and corporate support to prevail. When Moses hands were lifted, Israel prevailed and when they brought it down Amalek prevailed.

****

- As long as you burn like oil youll shine like light.

- Those who lose divine contact will never be connected and those who lose divine touch will never be remembered. So, keep the contact alive and always remember to keep in touch

- We know that God wants us to fighter because the Bible calls us soldiers.

- We are warriors. We are people of battle. We dont just receive medals from God. We earn them.
- If God didnt want you to fight, He would have given you the medal without the conflict. Stay in the fight.

# 8 INTERCESSORY PRAYERS EXEMPLIFIED

- **A sister whose husband left home** without any notice and stayed away for a long time. She thought the whole marriage had collapsed. I agreed with her in prayers that the man should be back in Jesus name. It looked like nothing would happen but a release was actually done in the Spirit that set the ball rolling. Obstacles were removed and roadblocks dismantled. The man was released and he came back and now more responsible and more of a father and a husband. Praise God.

- **Intercession should be made for those in authority** (1 Tim. 2:1-2), for all saints (Eph. 1:15-16), for those who forsake us, for enemies among whom we dwell, for kings, for all men (1 Tim. 2:1)

**Intercession in the Old Testament**

- **Abraham's Intercession for Sodom** (Genesis 18:23-33). Abraham interceded for God to spare a nation for the sake of the righteous there. He adduced strong reasons. God cannot destroy the wicked with the righteous. God agreed to Abraham's conditions. If 50 righteous were found, God would spare Sodom and Gomorrah. There were no fifty righteous. Then Abraham asked for 45 righteous. This failed and he asked for 40, reducing the number to 30, to 20 and finally to 10 righteous persons. God said for ten he will not destroy Sodom and Gomorrah

V. 32 Finally, Abraham inquired, "I hope my LORD will not be angry if I speak only once more. What if ten are found there?" He replied, "For the sake of those ten I won't destroy it." (ISV).

- **Abraham was regarded as a friend of God** because he was righteous. That is God trusted him enough to reveal his secret to him. God has secrets and cannot open up to talkative because he cannot trust them with secrets.

- when we pray do we intercede for others - for your family, for your pastor, for your government, for sinners to repent. We should not be selfish, thinking and praying for only our needs.

- **Moses Intercession** (because of the sin of the Golden Calf)

In the absence of Moses, the people chose another god outside Jehovah. A graven gold image. This drew the wrath of God and he wanted to wipe them out and create another nation but Moses interceded on their behalf.

### Ex. 32: 11- 14 AMP

11. But Moses besought the Lord his God, and said, Lord, why does Your wrath blaze hot against Your people, whom You have brought forth out of the land of Egypt with great power and a mighty hand?

12. Why should the Egyptians say, for evil He brought them forth, to slay them in the mountains and consume them from the face of the earth? Turn from Your fierce wrath, and change Your mind concerning this evil against Your people.

- **Daniel's Case** (Dan 9:1-3). Daniels Intercession for His People and for the Restoration of Jerusalem

### Dan 9:3 (AMP)

*And I set my face to the Lord God to seek Him by prayer and supplications, with fasting and sackcloth and ashes*

- During the reign of Darius Daniel uncovered the prophesy of desolation of Jerusalem. Read Daniel's intercessory prayer - vs 17-19. "Now therefore, O our God, listen to and heed the prayer of Your servant [Daniel] and his supplications, and for Your own sake cause Your face to shine upon Your sanctuary which is desolate.

O my God, incline Your ear and hear; open Your eyes and look at our desolations and the city which is called by Your name; for we do not present our supplications before You for our own righteousness and justice, but for Your great mercy and loving-kindness.

O Lord, hear! O Lord, forgive! O Lord, give heed and act! Do not delay, for Your own sake, O my God, because Your city and Your people are called by Your name."

### - Joshua's Intercession

(because of the sin of Achan and resultant defeat of Israel at Ai (Joshua 7:6-9).

V. 6 At this, Joshua tore his clothes, fell down to the ground on his face before the ark of the LORD until evening, he and the leaders of Israel and they covered their heads with dust (ISV)...

### God's Response:

V.11 Israel has sinned; they have transgressed My covenant which I commanded them. They have taken some of the things devoted [for destruction]; they have stolen, and lied, and put them among their own baggage.

V. 12. That is why the Israelites could not stand before their enemies, but fled before them; they are accursed and have become devoted [for destruction]. I will cease to be with you unless you destroy the accursed [devoted] things among you (AMP).

\*\*\*\*

- Those who never face opposition always stop at proposition. Those who never confront obstacles will always live with postponements and delays.


- When he landed here in 1848, there were no Christians, when he left in 1872 there were no heathens memorial to John Geddie


- The church began with men in the upper-room agonizing but today ending with men in the supper-room organizing. We started virile; we are ending sterile Leonard Ravenhill

# 9 INTERCESSION AND HEALING

- **The Gideonites** was the name of an intercessory prayer group I came to know. I discovered that God used this small group to pray for healing of the sick especially the barren. To the best of my knowledge any barren woman they prayed for became pregnant. This helped growth of the church. In the early 1970s worldwide revival there were lots of such small group prayer teams or prayer warriors geared towards solving specific problem area. Some prayed for world revival, some for salvation of souls, others for laborers into God's vineyard. What happened to this group that God used to help the body of Christ and churches? Today they are under attack or hijacked by the enemy. Some were derailed into some agenda not tailored to the good of the body of Christ. The church must return to her first love.

  - **The Scripture encourages us to intercede** for all types of groups and people. For the sick, widows and orphans, church leaders etc.

**James 5:14-15 (AMP)**

*Is anyone among you sick? He should call in the church elders (the spiritual guides). And they should pray over him, anointing him with oil in the Lord's name*

*And the prayer [that is] of faith will save him who is sick, and the Lord will restore him; and if he has committed sins, he will be forgiven.*

- **Sick system** (managers, politicians, people in place of authority). These are people in position of decision-making that affect all of us

**1 Tim 2:1-2 (ISV)**

Prayer and Submission to Authority

*1.First of all, then, I urge you to offer to God petitions, prayers, intercessions, and expressions of thanks for all people,*

*2. for kings, and for everyone who has authority, so that we might lead a quiet and peaceful life with all godliness and dignity.*

- Sometimes for individual intercessors, in reflective musical quietude offer your intercession. In this mood your prayers could come out in tears, moaning, groanings to God.

- **In many occasions I have found myself** in such mood where I wet my pillows with tears in distant strange land where duty had carried me to, praying for my people, for the sick, for friends I lost contact with, as if they were in that same room with me. Sometimes for hours I visualize their problems. I bear it with them in the presence of the Lord. Sometimes the holy spirit will give me the burden to pray for their needs. It could be a family, an individual, a church, a community, a people. Just flow along with the spirit. May God use you to be of help to someone in trouble, someone passing through a storm, a backslider.

- **One day a friend visited** and burst into real crying that people around ran into my room scared. What was the matter. A new convert had backslidden. He blamed himself as the new convert blamed him for not being around. That is the spirit of intercession, intercessory spirit. It comes with burden, groaning, penitential tears.

- **The target of the great commission** in Matthew 10:1,8 is to:

- *Heal the sick*
- *Cleanse the lepers*
- *Raise the dead*

- *Cast out devils*
- *Freely* (without pay) you have received, freely (without charge) give. That was and is still the command to us as a team of intercessors. In verse 10:1 Jesus gave us power of attorney, advocacy against unclean spirits, to cast them out, and to heal all manner of sickness and all manner of disease (Mk 16:15, 17-18, Mt 10:1, 7-8).

**- Healing, intercessory anointing** breaks the yoke of evil and sufferings, breaks yoke of physical, emotional, spiritual bondage.

**- Beloved stretch out in repentance** your healing hands to the heavens for restoration, for healing of life-threatening diseases, for healing stubborn haunting shadows of the past, and mend broken hearts.

****

- Catch the fire beloved and spread the flame. Let us redeem the time and let there be light in and around us.

- Hannah, the mother of Samuel, one of the most profound of intercessors, had no language. Her lips moved, but her voice was not heard. There is groaning that cannot be uttered. In the mountain-moving place of travailing prayers, linguists are not needed - Ravenhill

- The Lord regards not the grammar of prayers, how men word it in prayers; nor the arithmetic of prayers, how often they pray, nor the rhetoric of prayer, how finely they pray, nor the music of prayer, what sweetness of tone men have in prayer; but the divinity of groans. There are sighs and groaning, which cannot be uttered - Francis Raworth.

- He kept the iron red-hot with prayer, and God's skill fashioned it with enduring power. No man can do a great and enduring work for God who is not a man of prayer and no man can be a man of prayer who does not give much time to praying - E. M. Bounds.

# APPRECIATION

Thanks for finding time to read this. I hope you have been blessed. I will appreciate if you share this with your friends and write a customer review and rating down the book page online as it will help others share from this blessing too. Thanks so much and may Gods divine favor follow you. Would you like Amazon to notify you by email when I release a new book or the next book in any of the series? Then follow me directly at Amazon. Look for the large yellow Follow button on the left below my photo at this link below and click it.

http://www.amazon.com/author/ikechukwujoseph

Amazon won't give out your email address. God bless you and thanks for visiting. Expect more and bigger blessings.

# Discover other titles by Ikechukwu Joseph at Amazon.com:

## Fiction

The Last Curse (Angel Series Book One)
The Last Sacrifice (Angel Series Book Two)
Only You (Forever Series Book One)
Romance with Mother Shark (Forever Series Book 2)
The 12 Advocates (Forever Series Book 3)
-. Haunting Shadows (Book 1).
Stolen Conscience (Political Scavengers Series Bk 1)
Stolen Tomorrow (Political Scavengers Series Bk 2)

## Holy Spirit Series

- Holy Spirit Anointing: Vol. 1 Holy Spirit Series Bk. 1
-Holy Spirit Anointing: Vol. 2 – Holy Spirit Series Bk. 2
- Gifts and Ministries of the Holy Spirit- Holy Spirit Series Bk. 3
- Gifts and Ministries of the Holy Spirit- Holy Spirit Series Bk. 3 (Paperback)

## Covenant Right Series

- Divine Immunity
(Covenant Right Series Book 1)
-Divine Remembrance Your Divine Decoration
(Covenant Right Series Book 2)
-Unlocking God's Divine Favor
(Covenant Right Series Book 3)

## Faith Supplement Series

- Principles of the Dynamics of Faith (How Faith Works)
(Faith Supplement Series, book One)
- Heroes and Heroines of our Faith and types of Faith
(Faith Supplement Series, book Two)
-. Through Faith: Living an Overcoming Life
(Faith supplement Series Book Three)
## Spiritual Warfare Series
- Strategic Spiritual Warfare
(Spiritual Warfare Series Book 1)
- Strategic Spiritual Warfare
(Expanded Version) (Paperback)
- Lord Show Me Your Glory
(Spiritual Warfare Series Book 2)
-Pulling Down Satanic Strongholds
(Spiritual Warfare Series Book 3)
## Pauline Epistles Series
Studies in the Book of Colossians
(Pauline Epistles Series Bk 1)
Studies in the Book of Philippians
(Pauline Epistles Series Bk 2)
Studies in the Book of Ephesians
(Pauline Epistles Series Bk 3)
Studies in the Book of Galatians
(Pauline Epistles Series Bk 4)
Studies in the books of Titus and Philemon
(Pauline Epistles Series Bk 5)
Pauline Epistles Series (Books 1-5), Paperback
## Lesson for Leaders Series
- Jesus Christ: Beyond the Miracles The Character
(Lesson for Leaders Bk 1)
- Jesus Christ Our Example: The Exemplary Leader
(Lesson for Leaders Bk 2)
. The Complete Leader: Jesus Christ the Accomplished
Perfect Total Leader (Lesson for Leaders Bk 3)
## Achievers Best Guide Series
-. Achievers Handbook 1 (Achievers Best Guide Series
Book 1)

-. Achievers Handbook 2 (Achievers Best Guide Series Book 2)

-. Achievers Handbook 3 (Achievers Best Guide Series Book 3)

-. Achievers Handbook 4 (Achievers Best Guide Series Book 4

-. Achievers Handbook 5 (Achievers Best Guide Series Book 5)

## Children's Salvation Series

-. Salvation Colors
(Children's Salvation Series - Book One)

-. Children's Salvation Alphabets
(Children's Salvation Series Book 2)

-. Children's Salvation Alphabets
(Children's Salvation Series Book 2) Paperback

## Bible Faith Nuggets Series

- Bible Faith Nuggets Series Box Set
(A collection of five-books)

## Stand-alone

- Discovering Yourself

- Unlocking Closed Doors

- Knowledge, Understanding, Wisdom: The Tripartite Force in the Pursuit of Divine Access

-Discover, Uncover and Recover All: The ZikLag Experience

- Repositioning Yourself for Greater Success

Words of Wisdom
(A New Collection of African Proverbs)

Words of Wisdom
(A Collection of African Proverbs with Categorization and Meanings)

.

# Appendix A: Are You Born Again?

You must be born twice i.e. - the natural or biological birth and the spiritual birth before you can see the kingdom of God. You must be born again. Are you saved? If the Lord comes now, will you be taken to heaven? Is your name written in the book of life? Where will you go when you die - heaven or hell? Tell yourself the truth, and do something about your situation. Heaven is a prepared place and for prepared people. Hell is a prepared place and for unprepared people. Do you want to be born again? Then

1. Recognize yourself as a sinner

- For all have sinned and come short of the glory of God - Rom. 3:23.

- You are a sinner by birth for in sin did your mother conceive you- Psalm 51:5

- You are a sinner by choice for all we like sheep have gone astray. Isaiah 53:6; Rom.6:23.

2. Repent and believe in Jesus Christ

-Repent you therefore, and be converted that you sins may be blotted out, Act 3:19.

3. Confess your sins

-With Godly sorrow, confess your sins and tell God you are sorry. Ask him to forgive you all. 1 John.1:9.

4. Accept Jesus Christ into your heart.

Say this sinners Prayer - Lord Jesus, I thank you for forgiving me according to your word. Come into my heart. Be my savior and Lord. Remove my name from the book of death and write it in the book of life. By faith I believe I am saved, Amen.

Congratulations for your bold sincere decision and confession. Write me today so that I pray along with you. Join a living church near you where they preach the truth.

## Appendix B: Testimonies from Pastor Ikechukwu Josephs Ministry

-Ordinary Men with Extraordinary Power
-Common Men with Uncommon Results
-Usual Men with Unusual Anointing
-Weak Men with Mighty Deeds
-Unschooled Mortal Men with Immortal Visions and PhD-
Producing Life Histories

- Faiths miracle on wattpad about my book, Discovering Yourself - OMG! This is amazing. You should update more. This is just I don't know extraordinary. May the good Lord bless you. I'm in love already with this book.

- Misstmaria on wattpad about my book - Discovering Yourself - Wow!!!! This is incredible and how right you are. What a wonderful lesson here!! Thank you!

- Byron Walker - I really enjoyed the book (Strategic Spiritual Warfare). ByronWalker6 voted on Wattpad for Strategic Spiritual Warfare

- I Love reading although I took my time to read this book it is full of the anointing. Stayed up reading until i could not anymore, already daylight in morning - got some rest and woke up in the presence of God to worship that is how it impacted me.

The prayers in this book also stirred up a desire within me to see the answers to those prayers. I will read more books from this Author

He knows the scripture and speaks clearly and the

anointing backs him up all glory to God.

Go ahead read it youll be glad and you will be touch by the beautiful presence of the Holy Spirit awesome read and will re-read again. Everyone should read this book highly recommended (referring to Holy Spirit Anointing: Bible Faith Nuggets Series Book 5 )

-Rebecca Belardo (Georgia) -

- Thank you so much for this book. It just showed up on my Kindle when I was seeking a Word from The Lord. This truth is truly from The Lord THANK YOU SO MUCH. JUANITA. USA

- Rated 5 stars, It was so refreshing - By Jamar w Jackson

- Loved it. I learned a lot of things in this book. Wow it was Slender. Loved this book PRAISE God

- Five Stars by Gary Blakely, Format: Kindle Edition Verified Purchase

Great Book on the anointing, if you want to learn more

- Five Stars by Betty H

Great book, full of wisdom, awesome author/writer!

- By Smackeyon - Power packed and informative.

- Five Stars by Will Pearceon - Very good and enlightening.

- By Amazon Customer "Rosa lee Watson" rated Five Stars Love it.

- Greetings am so blessed while searching books on amazon came across your book the Holy Spirit Anointing Bible Faith nuggets book 5. I started reading and truly did not want to stop. Am at page 690 it has really lifted me up and am anticipating to finish reading it and looking to read other books. It has just brought an awakening and ministered to me deeply. Thank you for sharing the knowledge God has grace you with, God bless you Joseph. Attentive and embracing God's presence Prophetess Rebecca

- Merry Christmas Pastor Joseph, you have been a big blessing to me by your messages that I have been receiving. I have used them on my pulpit. God bless you and may he shower his blessings upon you.

Your brother Pastor E. A. [Kenya]

- Dear Pastor Joseph,

You have been of a great blessing to me so much. Your teachings are so encouraging and very powerful. I am praying for you so much. I have been getting your teaching materials and I have been asking myself where you are coming from? Which country? May God bless you so much.

Pastor N. O. O (Kenya).

- Dear pastor IK,

Thanks, so much for the inspirational messages you have been sending to me. They have been of a very great help. God will richly bless you. Pastor Benjam

- My name is Matthew. I received an e-mail that was not intended for me. But i see God's divine hand diverting it to me. It was not even addressed to me at all. it was sent to Veronica Argentina. I have been seeking Gods anointing on the ministry he has called me into. And i have realized before I even received your e-mail that i did not want to do this without Gods hand of anointing upon it. There are just too many people out there that are in ministry that have not been anointed and called with anointing. If I speak or lay hands on someone for healing and do not have Gods hand in it I would rather not even bother. As of late I have been just seeking a deeper relationship with Jesus and only ministering to those that the lord sets right in front of me. The Lord has given me a great burden for the broken heart and the captive to sin; my own heart is broken before the lord in this. When I was in Peru I tasted of this anointing and as i came back to the U.S. there remain a remnant of that anointing for a while. But last night i was asked to speak and it was just words without the power of the life of Christ in them, i have grieved throw the night and woke to find this e-mail that was not even intended for me. (N.B: Bible Faith Nuggets Serous Edition he received was on Davidic Anointing. Same time he was asking for anointing from God). I love the lord so much and want to serve him. He has done so much for me. I will never be able to repay him for his goodness. SEEKING GOD DIRECTION IN MY

LIFE AND WHAT HE WANT ME TO DO AND GO.
- G. M (U.S.A)
- AWESOME Book. I'm glad you allow God to speak thru you to tell me where I was off track and how I should now proceed and proceed through this journey. Thank You and may God continue to Bless You.
- D. Woodrow
Hi, Pastor Joe,
I am actually blessed with your newsletter, even though we have not been able to have time together whether physically or on net. Please keep the line hot, for the Lord is your strength.
Shalom. - O.J
Dear Pastor Joseph,
Thanks a lot for your words of inspiration and insight. May God richly bless you and the ministry to continue with the good work you are doing?
P. H
Thanks for your message. I wonder where you got this from. Keep the candle burning.
-E.V (yahoo mails)
Pastor Joseph,
Thanks for all the sweet messages you have been sending. This is to wish you the best of this glorious year. I want to let you know that the Good Lord will continue
to bless and uphold you
J. M (Nigerian)
Thank you, my brother. You are sent by God. I have started my fasting today and I am very encouraged by these messages. Are you in Africa or abroad?
N.O (South Africa)
I am very much happy to have received this wonderful Book from you. I thank you and I wish to say that there is nothing you could have done better for me then this Book you have sent to me. Oh, Pastor just the very few pages I have had the chance to read, I was tempted to say it was just me in the picture. I really am happy to have this Book. I

wish you all the best and I say stay blessed but like the little Oliver, I ask for more. Merry Christmas and a Happy New Year!

-D. J. N (GHANA)

Pastor Joseph,

You never, never cease to bless me. I loved the writing on the borrowed axe head! AMEN.AMEN. AMEN!!!!!! (full title of the Edition she referred to was Borrowed Axe-Borrowed Anointing)

-Pastor D. S (U.S.A)

This is truly an eye-opening message that came straight from the throne room of God. I passed it on so others may be blessed.

-Evangelist Valrie (U.S.A)

Beloved,

Thanks a million for this and others you've been sending. Theyve all blessed my heart.

Shalom. U.I (Nigeria)

I am not sure how I managed to get on your mailing list but thanks this was something God wanted me to hear (Referring to Bible Faith Nuggets).

LYN

Hi Pastor,

I was edified after reading this nugget, the almighty God give you more inspiration and knowledge of His word.

-CO. (U.S.A)

Dearly beloved,

Thanks for your beautiful and inspirational messages, they are so timely, may the lord continue to make space for you in this ministry, do please include your contact phone number, I like to speak with you. God bless you real good. Amen. I.E

Greetings Ikechukwu,

Blessings and greetings in Jesus precious name! Thank you for your letter and words of encouragement! May God use you for the establishment of His Kingdom in the earth, and establish truth and justice. The LORD reigns, let the earth be glad; let the distant shores rejoice. Remain blessed in HIM!

-Pastor S.A (Ukraine)

Dear Joe

Thanks for your love, and also thanks for sending me a good message that bless my soul, i enjoyed it. May the lord richly bless you, thank you so much.

REV. V. U. J (Nigeria)

Dear Pastor, good day in Jesus Name. I read your book but I see it that God want to give me Victory because what I have read so far describes my 11-year-old problem.

Kate (Nigeria)

I Praise the Lord for all you that have sent me, emails of encouragement. If I would express how it had made me feel, we would all be in tears.

-Evangelist Neal (U.S.A)

# ABOUT THE AUTHOR

**Pastor Ikechukwu Joseph,** the author of "Discovering Yourself" is a notable song writer, poet, author and the publisher of bestselling "Unlocking Closed Doors, Strategic Spiritual Warfare, Haunting Shadows, Studies in the Book of Colossians (a verse-by-verse analytical study commentary), Studies in the Book of Philippians (a verse-by-verse analytical study commentary) and Angels Go to War. He trained as a Science Educator, Biologist, System Engineer and Website Developer. He is a graduate of University of Ibadan (M. Ed), University of Port Harcourt (B. SC) and a duly accredited ordained Minister with Evangelistic Messengers Association International, Tennessee, U.S.A. Pastor Joseph served God under different organizations like The Scripture Union, Four Square Gospel Church, NIFES, Fellowship of Christian Students, Grace of God Mission, and Believers Gospel Mission before God led him into the Harvest field.

# AUTHOR'S CONTACT

Email:
tlwgom@yahoo.com
Telephone:
+2348035033228
+2348022957255
Website: http://ikechukwujoseph.com

###

Connect with Me Online
Sign up for our newsletter: http://eepurl.com/b_ouQn
Website: http://ikechukwujoseph.com
Twitter: http://twitter.com/ikechukwujosep1
Facebook: http://facebook.com/ikechukwu2joseph
Wattpad: http://wattpad.com/ikechukwu2joseph

Made in the USA
Middletown, DE
15 October 2023

40858882R00046